DIFFERENTIATION OF MOODS
AS A REFLECTION OF
EGO ORGANIZATION AND
PERSONALITY STYLE

LISTENING VERY, VERY CLOSELY AS
PATIENTS ANSWER ONLY FIVE QUESTIONS

Robert Charles Powell

North Charleston, SC:
CreateSpace Independent Publishing Platform, 2017
Copyright © 2017
Robert Charles Powell

ISBN-10: 1543094392
ISBN-13: 978-1543094398

First Edition: February 2017
10 9 8 7 6 5 4 3 2 1

Differentiation of Moods as a Reflection of
Ego Organization and Personality Style:
Listening Very, Very Closely as
Patients Answer Only Five Questions

Heuristics are simple decision strategies ...
basing decisions on only a few relevant predictors. ...
[We] outline those features of heuristics that
make them useful in health care settings.
These features include their surprising
accuracy, transparency, and wide accessibility,
as well as the low costs and
little time required to employ them. [1]
Julian N. Marewski, Gerd Gigerenzer

This essay discusses a heuristic diagnostic approach that is
supported by extensive clinical experience. [2] The focus here is not on
proving anything but on exploring the notion that when patients use, for
example, the terms "anxious," "depressed," "angry," "afraid" – and even
"hungry" – clinicians and others in the patients' lives do not necessarily
understand the nuances about what the patients are talking. The focus here
is on the conclusions that one clinician has drawn from listening very, very
closely to patients. [3]

Think about this for a moment: when someone mentions one of
these common momentary emotions or lingering mood states, on what
grounds should it be supposed that both of you are "using the same
language" – even if that someone's words appear to be like those used in

your native tongue? That both of you share the same words does not automatically mean that both of you share the same understandings of those words and the feeling states they represent. Furthermore, on what grounds should it be supposed that both of you draw distinctions between those common emotions – that both of you view hunger, anxiety, depression, anger, and fear as discrete emotions rather than amorphous ones? On what grounds should it be supposed that both of you view these phrasings as durable conceptions rather than as time-bound perceptions?

For the most part, this essay will not focus on the varying definitions of "emotion" versus "mood" versus "affect" versus "feeling" – which, historically, mostly have been efforts to distinguish between shorter term and longer term conditions. "Mood" will be used as the default term, as emphasis will be on enduring states and patients' conceptual understandings – or lack of conceptual understandings.

Let us set a developmental context. Newborn babies cry in almost identical fashions for each of these named conditions – hunger, anxiety, depression, anger, and fear – not to mention a few more, such as wetness and cold. In the best of all worlds, a baby's caretaker listens very, very closely, then begins to distinguish different discrete cries and to encourage the individual baby to develop unique cries – that is, a discrete conception of a cry for each aspect of what originally was just a perception of discomfort. This does not occur overnight, but, in the best of all worlds, the child develops – and is encouraged by nearby adults to develop – discrete durable conceptions of hunger, anxiety, depression, anger, and fear – that is, discrete durable conceptions covering multiple concrete passing perceptions of each of the specific emotions. Ours is not the best of all worlds. Mental health clinicians day by day encounter patients who cannot quickly and efficiently sort out what specific emotion is being experienced, who "owns" it, what options exist for responding to it, and what, if any, action best should be taken. If all this cannot be sorted out quickly and efficiently, there is a greater chance that the patient, to some degree, in some manner, will become overwhelmed by the situation. Furthermore, if all one perceives is an amorphous discomfort, then it makes sense, on some level, to squash down the feeling in a generic manner, through alcohol, street drugs, or some other nonspecific action.

Heuristically, a key task is for the clinician to listen very, very closely – to recognize early on the degree to which a patient does or does not possess the level of personality organization required for not becoming overwhelmed. For example, in an emergency, the more easily overwhelmed patient generally represents a greater clinical risk than the not so easily overwhelmed patient – and a clinician needs to grasp this without delay.

For the following discussion, non-identifiable clinical data – exactly five answers to exactly five questions – without the author's current access to any further data or conclusions – has been collected for over four decades, primarily for teaching purposes. [4] The following are the set-up comments plus the subsequent five relevant questions asked routinely of thousands of patients:

> I would like to ask you five very specific questions about your emotions. A lot of people have difficulty with these five questions, but just do the best that you can.
>
> **(1) Do you ever take a look at yourself and say,**
> **"Gee, I guess I must be hungry?"**
> If so, how would you KNOW that you were feeling
> hungry or getting hungry?
> That the feeling you were feeling
> must be hunger – and not something else?
>
> **(2) Do you ever take a look at yourself and say,**
> **"Gee, I guess I must be anxious?"**
> If so, how would you KNOW that you were
> anxious or getting anxious?
> that the feeling you were feeling
> must be anxiety – and not something else?

(3) Do you ever take a look at yourself and say,
   "Gee, I guess I must be depressed?"
   If so, how would you KNOW that you were
      depressed or getting depressed?
      that the feeling you were feeling
      must be depression – and not something else?

(4) Do you ever take a look at yourself and say,
   "Gee, I guess I must be angry?"
   If so, how would you KNOW that you were
      angry or getting angry?
      that the feeling you were feeling
      must be anger – and not something else?

(5) Do you ever take a look at yourself and say,
   "Gee, I guess I must be afraid?"
   If so, how would you KNOW that you were
      afraid or getting afraid?
      that the feeling you were feeling
      must be fear – and not something else?

That's it. Answers to those five questions make up the entirety of the data used in this discussion. Frequently a patient had to be coaxed to say a bit more – and then a bit more after that – with the question, "Anything else?"

If the patient stumbled on the hunger question, then it would be expanded to, "If you were being held captive in a totally dark cave, how would you finally figure out that the way you were feeling must be hunger?" If the patient stumbled on the anxiety question (eg, confusing anxiety with eagerness), then it would be expanded to, "If you were giving a speech before a very large crowd, how might you have felt while walking up to the podium?" Sometimes for the anger question it would help to have the question expanded to, "What might have been the earliest warning sign that you were about to become angry?" In all cases, emphasis was placed upon the word "KNOW" – so a prompting question might be phrased as, "How else would you KNOW?"

In the examples given below, the data have been chosen – a phrase from here, a phrase from there – primarily because of their distinctive or interesting nature. Surely that is not an unusual approach, as the annals of medical literature tend not to pull lessons from otherwise boring cases but from those that catch a clinician's attention. The goal here is to encourage clinicians to listen very, very closely for the unique answers – and the unique ways of answering – that frequently provide important information about how individual patients think and view the world.

Let us now look at some of the subsets of data, so that you might begin to appreciate how differently individual patients might respond to these five simple questions. Even before formally considering a probable diagnosis, no doubt you will notice differences in the quality of the answers

　　　– that some patients answer using percepts,
　　　　　while some others answer using concepts;

　　　– that some patients answer sparsely,
　　　　　while some others answer extensively;

　　　– that some patients answer with details that are
　　　　　　trite and supposed to be universal,
　　　　while some others answer with details that are
　　　　　　idiosyncratic and specific to themselves;

　　　– that some patients answer using intra-psychic phrases,
　　　　　while some others answer using physiologic phrases;

　　　– that some patients answer in what sounds like
　　　　　　an obsessive manner,
　　　　while some others answer in what sounds like
　　　　　　a histrionic manner;

– that some patients literally cannot relate to these questions at all.

At the end of reading this essay it is hoped that a clinician – or even a non-clinician – never again will consider phrases such as "I'm anxious," "I'm depressed," "I'm angry," and "I'm afraid" to be self-explanatory.

*****

I.

First, let us consider two sets of examples of answers favored by patients who probably have **normal/ neurotic personality**, including notable facility in forming concepts. [5]

a heavily intra-psychic answer:

hunger:	"All I can think about is food."
anxiety:	"My mind races and I have too many thoughts all at once. I have difficulty retrieving words."
depression:	"I start having negative thoughts – and thinking about past problems."
anger:	"My mind gets stuck on revenge. I can't think of anything else."
fear:	"I'm aware that I start exaggerating. There is something to be scared of, but I might be blowing the situation all of proportion."

a heavily physiologic answer:

hunger:	"My stomach growls. I might get a headache – especially in the back of my head. I might feel a little weak. Eventually I feel nausea."
anxiety:	"My palms get sweaty and my heart rate goes up. I might get some tightness in my chest. I pace."
depression:	"I withdraw. I don't want to do anything or see anyone or go anywhere. I want to stay in bed, but either I have trouble falling asleep or I wake up in the middle of the night. My appetite drops."

anger: "I see red. I feel myself getting hot. I raise my voice. It's like an adrenalin feeling that I get."

fear: "I feel my heart rate go up and maybe my stomach drops. I start looking around a lot. My eyes open up. I feel I need to find a bathroom."

In each of the above two sets of examples
the answers *directly address the question of how does the patient personally KNOW when the specific mood is present*;
the answers also *tend to use the words "I" and "my" a lot.*

That is, such patients are comfortable stating how they uniquely know – regardless of how others might or might not know – and there is an ownership of the mood. Each of these patients *has a clear, personal concept of each mood.* **Their moods may be described as "well differentiated".**

Sometimes a patient will *address one of the questions with a good-quality answer but will address the remainder with poor-quality answers* (those not addressing how the patient does KNOW – see below). In such cases, it usually turns out that the person has been in some variety of psychotherapy – or self-help or similar conscious process – addressing problems with that one mood that now is better grasped and better controlled. For example, a patient who really loved his job was warned directly by his boss that either he would learn how to control his anger or he would be fired. This highly motivated patient checked out several library books about anger and taught himself how to control that one of his moods.

Sometimes a patient will do the opposite – *address one of the questions with a poor-quality answer but will address the remainder with good-quality answers* (those addressing how the patient does KNOW – see below). In such case, it usually turns out that the missing area of knowledge concerns a mood that was experienced in an above average manner – or in a below average manner – or both – in the patient's childhood and adolescence. For example, if the patient was raised in an environment full of uncontrolled anger – or of never mentioned anger – or both – then the patient probably does not have an effective grasp of anger and its modulation. That is, the patient probably does not grasp that discrete amounts of anger – "small, medium, or large" amounts – might be appropriate responses to a given problem. Similar situations hold when one of the patient's parenting adults used anxiety or depression in response to almost everything while another parenting adult either denied or ignored the overused mood. [6] Occasionally the patient will report having had such parenting adults but nonetheless seems to have a rather good grasp of the mood in question. In such a case, it pays to ask, "Who else helped to raise you?" – where upon the examiner frequently discovers that a grandparent, an older sibling, a neighbor, a teacher, or some other relatively normal/neurotic person actually was the most important influence in the patient's life. The following are some examples of one *really poor – almost non-existent and generally ineffective – response*:

hunger:	"I don't know. I'd feel different inside."
anxiety:	"I wouldn't be anxious. I've never been anxious."
depression:	"I'm not sure. I'd have to think about that. I don't feel right. How would I know? I can just tell."
anger:	"Something provokes it. I can sense it."
fear:	"You just feel it. Anyone would feel that way."

Frequently a patient will *offer relatively good-quality answers, but one or more answers focus mostly on what action the person takes upon sensing that the mood is present – what might be called a "treatment" response*. It is as if the emotion has been sufficiently overwhelming in the past that the person has developed a method for squashing down the emotion almost before consciously acknowledging its presence. The following are some examples of *a treatment response*, focused on action:

hunger:	"I just eat. That's all there is to it."
anxiety:	"Maybe I'll start pacing around – or shoot some dope. Sometimes I take a really deep breath."

depression:	"Mostly I go to bed and stay there. Maybe I end up drinking a lot of beer. I try to find a laugh."
anger:	"I'd be punching the wall or someone until the anger calmed down. I'd pour water on my head."
fear:	"Run. I'd just run. I'd back away and hide."

Occasionally a patient will *provide an extensive answer – what might be called* **an "expert" response** *–* which raises the question of why the patient has spent a lot of time thinking about that one specific mood. A very specific example is when a patient provides *notably good answers regarding BOTH anger and fear.* Not always – but almost always – *this pattern correlates with a history of early childhood trauma.* When this pattern is found, a good follow-up question would be, "As far as you remember or have been told, did anything out of the ordinary happen during the first four years of your life?" Sometimes the patient might reveal something that happened at age five or so, but usually the response concerns an early event during which the child probably sensed that showing either anger or fear only would make the situation worse. The event might have been sudden parent loss or surgery or rape – or something similarly overwhelming. Sometimes the missing information comes out at the next session, once the patient has had time to think further about the question and to bring the answer out of repression. The following are some examples of **an expert response**:

hunger:	"If I have too much sugar then I get irritable and angry – and maybe have nightmares. If I'm really, really hungry then I get headaches, mostly at the back of my head."
anxiety:	"My mind would get dizzy. My equilibrium would be off. My heart pounds. I'd feel like I might fall down because my legs are shaky. My seeing would be blurred and my eyes are twitching. My stomach would be tight and I'd feel really sick. I have to get away from everybody."

depression:	"I feel shut down, separated from everything and everyone. I want to detach and be non-existent. I don't see the point of my life or anybody's life. I don't know what to do with myself. Eventually I start to cry."
anger:	"I feel like getting violent – like having tantrums. I get hot. It's like smoke is coming out of my ears – like I'm burning – and then I go crazy."
fear:	"I have a ton of dreams about fear – about people trying to attack me. In these dreams I feel like I'm going to die – and I have to convince these guys not to kill me. This happens almost every night – for years. It's as if everyone out there knows me – but I know they don't. I get sort of paralyzed and my mind starts to think life is over."

Sometimes a patient does the exact opposite of offering an expert response, providing what might be called **a "denial" response** – denying ever having – or having had – this or that mood at all. Such an answer is surprisingly common – and might be offered for a variety of reasons.

Occasionally a patient will provide a somewhat unusual answer that nonetheless addresses "how would you KNOW?" – what might be called **an *"idiosyncratic"* response**. While most patients learn "at mother's knee," so to speak, to differentiate their moods – to associate this or that set of specific percepts with this or that specific mood term, a concept – some patients – frequently those of quite good intelligence – puzzle out the associations on their own. Rather than having learned the differentiations during constant banter (hearing plus talking) between the child and a parenting adult, such patients seem to have learned primarily through hearing alone or through their own solitary experience. When this pattern is found, a good follow-up question would be, "Were there a lot of children in your family at the time you were born?" If the patient's was not such a large family, then one might wonder if the patient was raised in an orphanage or is somewhat autistic. The following are some examples of *an idiosyncratic response*:

hunger:	"It's kind of a hot feeling in my stomach and my jaw starts to hurt."
anxiety:	"My skin gets bad and I start dreaming of flying."
depression:	"I'm constantly wanting to be on the phone. It's like my body sinks to my feet."
anger:	"I say a lot to myself. My mind twirls."
fear:	"It's a great feeling, like when a tornado comes! My heart feels shaky."

Clearly the above answers probably are not ones the patients learned through conversations with someone else.

Another factor to consider with these five questions is that a patient's responses might be predominantly *paranoid/ schizoid/ antisocial* in tone, predominantly *obsessive/ dependent/ avoidant* in tone, or predominantly *narcissistic* in tone. Intriguingly, those who probably have *histrionic* personality tend to provide good quality answers – at arms' length – as if describing a neighbor rather than themselves. Through listening very, very closely to patients as they answer these five specific questions, quite a lot can be learned.

*****

II.

Second, let us consider four sets of examples of answers favored by patients who probably have **borderline personality**, including some degree of difficulty in forming concepts. [7]

universalization:

hunger:	"Your stomach tells you that you want food. You think about food a lot. Your stomach gets tight. You get a cramp in your stomach. You just get naturally hungry. You feel empty."

anxiety:	"It's like your head is in a vise. You get this tingly, sick feeling."
depression:	"You know, you just don't feel normal. You know: everyone knows what it's like to feel depressed."
anger:	"Your fists get ready to hit someone. You just feel it come over yourself."
fear:	"You just want to run."

externalization:

hunger:	"If I'm noticing food, then I guess I must be hungry. If it's lunch time, I eat. The clock tells me I'm hungry."
anxiety:	"When my friends tell me to stop tapping my fingers, then I know I must be anxious."
depression:	"My house will show it. If it is a total mess – all dusty – then probably I'm depressed. Sometimes I can look in the mirror and tell that I'm depressed."
anger:	"People tell me I look angry."
fear:	"Usually I don't, but my close friends recognize that I'm afraid. They get me out of there and then tell me about it."

overlapping:

hunger:	"I eat when I'm angry."
anxiety:	"I think anxiety and depression are kind of the same. In each case I just want to cry."
depression:	"I get violent. That seems sort of odd, but I do. I lash out and later maybe I'll figure out that I was depressed."
anger:	"Usually I don't recognize that I'm angry, but then, if I do, I get depressed and afraid about having been angry and about what trouble maybe

	that's going to cause me. Sometimes I just get anxious." [anger "causing" anxiety is common]
fear:	"Usually it's mixed up with anger, but I talk about the fear rather than the anger. I overcome fear with anger. Whichever, mostly I freeze."

concrete example:

hunger:	"Let's see. This morning at first I thought I had a stomach ache but then I decided it must be hunger."
anxiety:	"Your questions keep going around and around in my mind. Sometimes that happens, I think, if I'm anxious."
depression:	"I was crying before I came here, so that must be depression. My sister says she cries when she is depressed."
anger:	"Yesterday I threw a brick. I remember clenching my fists and pacing – and then I just threw that brick."
fear:	"Right now I'm sort of frozen up. That's probably fear."

Such patients tend to use
universalization ("you," "your," "everybody");

> that is, they assume that everyone in the world formulates moods in exactly the same way – and, indeed, that there is one correct way to respond; quite commonly they will comment that – and want verification that – such and such is the "normal" response. [Interestingly enough, such patients also tend to describe others in similarly stereotyped non-useful ways: "My mother is nice – and funny – sometimes helpful. She's just a normal mother. My father is the same: helpful, nice, funny – just like anybody else's father." That is, just as the patient tends not to have a clear, discrete concept of this or that specific mood, the patient tends not to have a clear, discrete concept of a specific other person. As an

augmentation of the five mood questions, an examiner can ask, "Tell me about the folks who raised you" – or "Tell me about one or two of your closest friends – what each is like as a person".] [In regard to hunger, the answer "You feel empty" is common enough for one to note that it correlates with the lack of any vision of the future. A good follow-up question would be, "Where do you see yourself in ten years?" Almost invariably the patient answers with some variety of "I don't know".]

Such patients tend to use
externalization;

> that is, they rely on indicators outside themselves as to how they might be feeling.

Such patients tend to use
overlapping;

> that is, they tend to use the same answer for several of the mood questions. [This kind of conceptual confusion frequently parallels identify confusion.]

Such patients tend to use
*concrete example*s;

> that is, they tend to try, so it seems, to create a concept on the spot from recent percepts.

In each of the above four sets of examples
the answers ***only indirectly address the question of how does the patient personally KNOW when the specific mood is present***;
the answers also *tend to use the words "you" and "your" a lot*.

That is, such patients are NOT comfortable stating how they uniquely know – and want to be assured that this or that answer is "normal". Each of these patients *has a fuzzy, impersonal notion of each mood. **Their moods may be described as "poorly differentiated"**.*

*****

III.

Third, let us consider several sets of examples of answers favored by patients who probably have **psychosis or pre-psychosis**, including some definite difficulty in forming concepts.

> hunger: "I don't know. I guess I just eat out of habit. I was hungry this morning maybe. You ought to know when you're hungry."
>
> anxiety: "I wouldn't know how to answer that. Mostly I don't allow myself to have emotions."
>
> depression: "I've never been depressed. For some people, it just comes. I think anyone would know when they are depressed. It's like a feeling."
>
> anger: "You're not supposed to get angry. I did get angry last night when my sister stole my pizza. That's an interesting question."
>
> fear: "I wake up with it, but I really couldn't tell you what it's like. Some people get afraid of what people think about them."

Such patients tend to become
very uncomfortable with these questions –

> probably because they sense that they have no idea how to answer them.

Such patients tend to be
unable to address the question of
how they KNOW that a certain mood is present –

> probably because much of the time these relatively disturbed – even disorganized – patients do not know what is going on inside of themselves or during their interactions with others.

Such patients tend toward
denying ever experiencing this or that mood at all.

As noted above, the set-up for these five questions includes the phrase, "A lot of people have difficulty with these questions, but just do the best that you can" – as a kind of gentle warning that the patient might become uncomfortable with the questions. For the same reason, the five questions proceed from the least emotionally charged question – about hunger (which picks up issues of desire) – to the most emotionally charged question – about fear. It is not uncommon at all for such a psychotic or pre-psychotic patient to begin pacing around the interview room or to walk out. The five questions literally "do not compute," so such a patient does not want others to know that he or she cannot grasp the meanings of the questions at all.

Occasionally a psychotic or pre-psychotic patient who nonetheless has a high intelligence quotient will answer by using the specific mood term in a sentence – while not really addressing the question of how he or she might KNOW that the specific mood indeed is present. At times, it seems as if the patient is trying to remember a recent concrete situation and then, so to speak, to create, however unsuccessfully, a crude concept on the spot. The following are some examples of such "socially correct" responses from those who deal primarily with percepts rather than concepts:

hunger:	"A lot of people get hungry, and then they just eat."
anxiety:	"Somehow I'd know. If I was anxious right now, maybe I'd know."
depression:	"I've heard of people who said they were depressed."
anger:	"My sister talks about anger all the time, so I guess she knows what it is."
fear:	"It's like a feeling. Maybe that's why I drink?"

In each of the above sets of examples
the answers *do NOT directly address the question of how does the patient*

personally KNOW when the specific mood is present;
the answers also tend to suggest tangentiality or free association – and to induce some degree of initial frustration in the questioner.

That is, such patients are NOT comfortable at all being asked these questions – let alone stating how they uniquely know this or that mood. Each of these patients *lacks even a fuzzy notion – let alone a concept – of each mood.* ***Their moods may be described as "undifferentiated".*** [8]

As noted above, such data – exactly five answers to exactly five questions – has been collected on newly evaluated patients for over four decades. Around 1979 or so, the set-up comments and these five questions were printed out as the "Powell Differentiation of Mood Queries" ("PDMQ"). For over a decade, such information routinely was collected in the presence of medical students or psychiatric residents in training – who generally were startled by some of the forthcoming answers, as they erroneously assumed that just about everyone grasped hunger, anxiety, depression, anger, and fear as they did. The frequently unexpected answers certainly encouraged trainees to listen very, very closely to patients – and to avoid quickly accepting patients' presenting pronouncements about suffering from "anxiety," "depression," "anger," "fear," or some other self-diagnosed condition.

One enormously important aspect of the five questions – the PDMQ – is that the patient being evaluated probably never before has been quizzed about the mood assertions he or she made with previous examiners. Patients all the time declare that they are "anxious" or "depressed" or "angry" or "afraid" – but that does not mean that the patients and their examiners share the same understandings of those words and the feeling states they represent. It also does not mean that both parties draw distinctions between those common emotions – that both view hunger, anxiety, depression, anger, and fear as ***discrete moods*** rather than as amorphous ones. Furthermore, it does not mean that both parties view these phrasings as ***durable conceptions*** rather than as time-bound perceptions.

These five specific questions rapidly provide valuable information suggesting the patient's probable level of ego-organization: normal/ neurotic, borderline, or psychotic/ pre-psychotic. In a crisis – for example, in the emergency room – such information is crucial for evaluating the level of risk for uncontrolled or disorganized behavior. The correlation is not perfect, but think about this for a moment: who is more likely to kill him- or herself or others?

> someone who has clear awareness of anger, clear ownership of it, some understanding of why it is there, and some grasp of options for handling it? – or
> someone who has a confused awareness, ambivalent ownership, fuzzy understanding, and somewhat limited grasp of options? – or
> someone who is overwhelmed by a mixture of emotions, unclear about who owns the emotions, unclear about why the emotions are there, and unable to entertain options?

That is, who is most likely to kill him- or herself or others?
> someone who most likely has
> > a normal/ neurotic personality structure? – or
> someone who most likely has
> > a borderline personality structure? – or
> someone who most likely has
> > a psychotic or pre-psychotic personality structure?

Clearly it would be best to know a lot more about the patient, but sometimes a rapid assessment of risk must be made.

These five specific questions – the PDMQ – help an examiner to sort out quickly and efficiently who most likely would be able to maintain control over disruptive mood and who most likely would not. To revisit the opening quotation from Marewski and Gigerenzer:

Heuristics are simple decision strategies ...
basing decisions on only a few relevant predictors. ...
[We] outline those features of heuristics that
make them useful in health care settings.
These features include their surprising
accuracy, transparency, and wide accessibility,
as well as the low costs and
little time required to employ them. [1]

Julian N. Marewski, Gerd Gigerenzer

Many patients – especially fairly intelligent ones – or ones who have been examined psychiatrically many times – can fake some degree of normalcy for a while – especially with an inexperienced examiner – but these five rather unexpected questions tend to bring important information to the surface very quickly. While the time employed will vary from patient to patient, generally it takes about seven minutes to administer the five questions and to listen very, very closely to the answers. [9]

This essay discussed a heuristic diagnostic approach that is supported by extensive clinical experience. The focus here was not on proving anything but on exploring the notion that when patients use, for example, the terms "anxious," "depressed," "angry," "afraid" – and even "hungry" – clinicians and others in the patients' lives do not necessarily understand the nuances about what the patients are talking. The focus here was on the conclusions that one clinician has drawn from listening very, very closely to patients.

This heuristic diagnostic approach suggests that a patient's capacity for differentiation of moods might serve as a reflection of that patient's ego organization and personality style. A psychometrically validated approach to this data would be welcomed. In the meantime, perhaps the PDMQ can be viewed as a useful clinical tool.

*****

Endnotes:

1.　　Marewski JN, Gigerenzer G. "Heuristic decision making in medicine." Dialogues Clin Neurosci. 2012 Mar;14(1):77–89, p.77; http://www.ncbi.nlm.nih.gov/pubmed/22577307

2.　　The opening formulation of the situation follows that used by Harley C. Shands. "An Approach to the Measurement of Suitability for Psychotherapy." Psychiat Q. Sep 1958;32(3):500-521; reprinted in his Semiotic Approaches to Psychiatry, The Hague, Mouton, 1970, pp.150-171. One could say that this current long overdue essay had its origins in September-November 1968 when I first made contact with Dr. Shands (1916-1981) plus during January-March 1973 that this author "apprenticed" under him. At the time, he was perhaps the leading linguistic/ semiotic psychiatrist in North America, if not the world. He and I had an unusual but rather productive relationship. In addition to watching him interview patients, I had full run of his extensive files – which included a number of draft and otherwise unpublished manuscripts. I would choose an interesting proto-article, heavily edit it, and then place it on his desk at the end of the day. The next morning, he would attack the old manuscript with "new eyes" – generally with great creative energy and enthusiasm – adding bits and pieces of new insight. Then I would edit the improved manuscript again. We "danced this dance" over and over, such that I learned a lot about his thinking and he got a lot more manuscripts into publication. There is no question that Shands was brilliant – or that he worked well with an editor.

　　　Sometime around 1979 – maybe earlier – I put together the formal set of questions that I called the "Powell Differentiation of Moods Queries" (PDMQ). Clearly, these were based on what I learned from Shands (see Shands, 1960, and Shands, 1976-77, noted below). I used this approach – I still use this approach – with every patient evaluated and I taught the five questions to a number of other clinicians, especially students and resident physicians. Early in the game – around 1983, as I recall – an effort was made to correlate the pattern of the five answers with the pattern of a patient's Rorschach test results. For logistic reasons, the effort fell by the wayside, but my clinical colleague definitely sensed that the PDMQ provided a "quick and dirty" – heuristic – diagnostic approach for ascertaining level of ego organization and somewhat of personality style.

Just about everything written by Shands is highly recommended. To say that his writings are a bit mind boggling would be somewhat of an understatement. ["semiotics" is the study of patterned communication in all modalities]

Shands HC. Thinking and Psychotherapy: An Inquiry into the Processes of Communication. Cambridge, Harvard University Press, for the Commonwealth Fund, 1960 (reprinted by the publisher, 2013); several sentences appearing late in the book include kernels of what developed as the approach outlined in the current essay:

p.240. "The less complex person reports that he is nervous or fidgety; he seeks to demonstrate what he means by referring to the experience of the examiner ('you know what it's like to be nervous, don't you?') or of his group ('I feel just like anybody that feels nervous')."

p.276. "Often ... if one asks a concrete thinker how he knows he is angry or frightened, he will resort to saying, 'How does anybody know he's angry?' implicitly assuming that this is a revelation common to all men."

Consider also Shands' following comments:

p.10. "only when the participants are quite sure that their words have essentially the same meaning can the language be confidently employed for communication within the social unit."

p.115. "It is only through description that one can discover what is 'conscious' to someone else; 'conscious' is therefore synonymous with describable." [That is, if the person cannot describe the mood state, then maybe the person is not truly conscious of it as a concept.]

p.118. "Persons with emotional disorders have as well intellectual disorders ...." [That is, they have intellectual disorders relating to the formation and use of concepts.]

p.205. "the degree to which anything is known is identical with the ability to describe it ...."

Shands HC. Semiotic Approaches to Psychiatry. The Hague, Mouton, 1970.

Shands HC. The War with Words, Structure and Transcendence. The Hague, Mouton, 1971.

Shands HC, Meltzer JD (1946-xxxx). Language and Psychiatry. The Hague, Mouton, 1973.

Shands HC. "Disability, psychosomatic disease, and psychoneurosis: the problem of differential vulnerability." Psychother Psychosom. 1976-77;27:179-184; Shands discussed patients who were "unable to form abstract categories" and patients who had an "inability to 'know' ... inner feelings"; Shands frequently cited the following: Dewey J, Bentley A. Knowing and the Known. Boston, Beacon Press, 1949.

Shands HC, Meltzer JD. "Unexpected semiotic implications of medical inquiry." in Sebeok T, ed. A Perfusion of Signs. The Hague, Mouton, 1977; pp.77-89.

Shands HC. Speech as Instruction: Semiotic Aspects of Human Conflict. The Hague, Mouton, 1977.

Shands HC, Meltzer JD. "Verbal patterns and medical disease: prophylactic implications of learning." In Sebeok T, ed. Sight, Sound, and Sense. Bloomington, Indiana University Press, 1978; pp.175-201.

Bär E [later he spelled his last name "Baer"]. Semiotic Approaches to Psychotherapy. The Hague, Mouton, 1975; pp.81-105 discusses Shands' contribution toward increasing the scientific status of psychiatry; I read an early draft of the manuscript during my time apprenticing with Shands in 1973. Much to my later surprise, Bär credits me personally on p.120 for drawing his attention to certain aspects of Jurgen Ruesch's work.

The following doctoral dissertation also is recommended for consultation in that the opening chapters summarize quite well the available literature on the topic of how mood differentiation relates to emotional regulation:

Kanagy C. Field Independence, Somatic Awareness, Autonomic Arousal, and Emotion Differentiation as Predictors of Emotion Regulation. Unpublished PhD dissertation, Chapel Hill: Department of Psychology (Clinical Psychology), University of North Carolina at Chapel Hill, 2008; on the internet at
https://cdr.lib.unc.edu/indexablecontent/uuid:720f1677-dce0-436a-a793-40cfe5d40268

p.ii. "A thread of the growing literature on emotion and emotion regulation aims at understanding the psychological processes an individual uses to regulate emotion, and at identifying what characteristics and abilities are conducive to efficient emotion regulation. These studies have produced a growing list of emotion regulation correlates suggesting that a quality of self-awareness, the tendency to be attentive to self rather than surroundings, the ability to understand one's feelings precisely, and recently the very specific ability to put exact words to one's feelings are all positive predictors of emotion regulation. ... We hypothesized that this ability to differentiate emotional states would lead to improved overall emotion regulation. ... "

p.18. "*Emotion differentiation and emotion regulation*. Emotion differentiation is defined as the ability to clearly distinguish one emotion from another; to be able to recognize and state one's feelings precisely. ... Individuals who show high levels of emotion differentiation tend also to have more information about their emotions; specifically, they are more likely to be aware of the cause, context, physiological symptoms, and potential means of regulation of an individual emotion than an individual with a lower level of differentiation (Mesquita & Frijda, 1992; Schwarz & Clore, 1983; Shweder, 1993). Conversely, undifferentiated feelings assigned only a valence (positive or negative) and intensity provide the individual with little information about how best to deal with the emotion and the circumstances causing it (Schwarz & Clore, 1983, 1996).

Studies of mood differentiation are limited but informative. Swinkels & Giuliano (1995) studied individuals they called "mood labelers" those individuals more able to precisely define their moods, and "mood monitors" those individuals more likely to monitor the intensity of their moods."

p.19. "Feldman, Barrett et al. (2001) examined the relationship between emotional differentiation and emotion regulation by evaluating subjects' emotion journals for levels of emotion differentiation; this level of emotion differentiation was then compared to self-reports of emotion regulation. They found that emotion differentiation correlated significantly with regulation for negative but not for positive emotion, and pointed to the results of Schwarz & Clore (1983) suggesting that in our culture, negative emotions are more subject to regulation than are positive emotions."

3.   Regarding the benefits of listening very, very closely to patients, see also my booklet that explores the correlation of patients' presenting complaints with later documented iron deficiency (especially in men), pyridoxine (B-6) deficiency, zinc deficiency, severe vitamin D deficiency, definite hypercalcemia, definite magnesium deficiency, cobalamin (B-12) deficiency, and definite hypocalcemia.

Powell RC. Erroneous psychiatric self-diagnosis: non-psychiatric patients that present at a psychiatrist's office. available on Amazon through Kindle & through North Charleston, SC: CreateSpace Independent Publishing Platform, May 2015.

4.   Each set of answers in this essay is composed of bits and pieces of responses from multiple unidentified patients. The answers are meant to serve as mere examples of phenomena.

"SACHRP [The Secretary's Advisory Committee on Human Research Protections, US Health & Human Services] believes that research involving these types of data [masses of previously-collected non-identifiable data] provides a significant opportunity for generating beneficial knowledge for society, that research using already-collected data is often of minimal risk, and that concerns about protection of personal privacy are best dealt with by emphasizing stringent conditions on security and use, rather than by disapproving and preventing the research. In general, the use of real world data (and of previously-

collected research data) for research should be encouraged based on this risk-benefit profile, with appropriate attention to concerns about privacy and respect for autonomy." October 2014.
http://www.hhs.gov/ohrp/sachrp-committee/charter/index.html#

"Clinical research and the HIPAA privacy rule." NIH Publication Number 04-5495. February 2004. "Attachment A: Human subjects research implications of 'big data' studies." "The Privacy Rule permits a covered entity to use or disclose PHI [personal health information] for research under the following circumstances and conditions: ... If the PHI has been de-identified in accordance with the standards set by the Privacy Rule at section 164.514(a)-(c) (in which case, the health information is no longer PHI)."
https://privacyruleandresearch.nih.gov/clin_research.asp

5.   The following article is recommended for consultation in that it summarizes quite well some important points about the abilities and inabilities of those with borderline personality or with schizophrenia to form concepts:

Vulević G, Opačić G. "The role of cognitive-developmental tests in differential diagnosis of borderline and schizophrenic patients." Psihologija. 2012;45(2):139-154;
http://www.doiserbia.nb.rs/img/doi/0048-5705/2012/0048-57051202139V.pdf

p.140. "As far as the problem of concreteness is concerned, Vygotsky's research of this topic, although it was done decades ago, is still relevant and potentially useful in modern clinical psychology (Vygotsky, 1934). By using his Concept Formation Test, Vygotsky put his patients into a situation which compelled them to form new, artificial concepts. ... The results showed that schizophrenic patients were not able .... to form a concept. Instead, they formed complexes – collections of objects that relate to each other in a concrete, factual way."

p.144, "Sincrets (disorderly, disorganized groups without any structure in which it is difficult to perceive the criteria used to classify the objects)."

p.146. "Table 2 shows the achievements of the subjects at Vygotsky Concept Formation Test. The results clearly indicate statistically significant differences between the groups: normal subjects form concepts, half of borderline patients were not able to form concepts (they formed complexes), while schizophrenic patients predominantly formed complexes, about a third of them formed sincrets, while only one subject was able to form a concept."

p.151. "The results at Vygotsky Concept Formation Test suggest that an inability to form concepts could be considered one of the important indicators of SCH [schizophrenia]."

p.152. "Our results showed that half of the patients with BPD [borderline personality disorder] did not form concepts, but complexes."

6.   On many occasions across the decades a child's or adolescent's answers could be compared to the answers provided by one or both parents. As might be expected, if the youngster had problems handling a specific mood question, frequently a parent did, too – as a parent cannot teach what a parent does not know. It can be quite helpful to guide such a family toward developing a shared vocabulary about moods.

A related phenomenon was noted with couples who were having relationship problems. Take, for example, the question about "depression" or the question about "anger" as answered independently by each party: *if one gave a good-quality answer while the other gave a poor-quality answer*, then they literally were not "using the same language". Again, it can be quite helpful to guide such a couple toward appreciating their discrepancies in grasping and communicating moods.

7.   The categories "universalization," "externalization," "overlapping," and "concrete example" are my own – developed around 1979 – maybe earlier. Through listening very, very closely to patients others had diagnosed as having borderline personality, these categories came to mind. It would not surprise me at all to learn that the distinction of these categories developed in my mind after discussions with Shands and reading of his articles. In writing this manuscript over four decades

after having been with Shands, this author is trying to sort out which ideas are his and which were from the mentor.

In his "An Approach to the Measurement ... (1958/ 1970), Shands does note that "Not only do 'difficult' patients tend to use more distant words in describing feelings, but they also tend to speak of themselves while using pronouns appropriate to others. ... This method of expressing oneself rests upon an assumption that the experience of every human being is identical with that of every other one" (p.162 in 1970). "The use of inappropriate pronouns merges into the use of generalizations such as 'everybody," "anybody," and 'they'.... Such a patient talks about what 'they' are going to do, and it is impossible to get him [or her] to describe the referent to this plural pronoun" (p.163 in 1970). "They take the occurrence of states of emotion for granted, but they presume that these states are common to everyone; and they tend to be evoked, not by a description from 'inside," but rather by reference to the stimulus. The patient implicitly assumes that there is a standard response to a given stimulus ..., and that to refer to the situation is enough to define the emotional response" (pp.165-166 in 1970). "A leading characteristic of this system or frame of reference is its assumed universal validity. ... The unconscious assumption is that one person's experience is similar to another's, that all human beings have (or at least should have) the same sort of values ... (p.167 in 1970). In his "Verbal Patterns and Medical Disease ..." (1978), Shands does note "the assumption that 'my feelings' are the same as those of 'everyone' and therefore need not be described ..." (p.197). Thus, Shands does not summarize all this as "universalization" – but clearly this author's notion may well come from the mentor's observations as well as his own.

Regarding this author's notion of "externalization," Shands does note that for such patients "[internal] feelings are ... inferred as a necessary extrapolation from his [or her] over [external] behavior" (p.181 in 1978). Thus, again, this author's notion may well come from the mentor's observations as well as his own. In Shands' articles, this author has not come across anything like his own notions of "overlapping," and "concrete examples". Shands' comment that these patients "cannot differentiate accurately" may have influenced the choice of a title for the current essay

– especially in that Shands had a long-standing habit of mulling over his ideas long before getting them published (p.181 in 1978).

8.   In their "Unexpected semiotic implications ..." (1977), Shands and Meltzer comment, "The psychiatrist *expects* to find anxiety, depression, or anger, and in working in psychotherapy with 'neurotic' patients this expectation is routinely validated. It comes as a surprise to try to explore 'feelings' of this sort, especially with reference to the 'inner' correlates of visceral and proprioceptive sensations, only to encounter complete incomprehension on the part of the person interviewed in response to questions about such feeling state. As one listens carefully to many [non-neurotic] interviewees in this manner, it becomes clear that the expectation held by ... [such patients] is that emotional states are so standard that they do not need to be described. If the interviewer asked about feelings corresponding to postures or facial expressions exhibited, the ... [patient] may agree that he feels 'angry,' but in answer to the question as to *how* that feeling is known, the answer is likely to be, 'The same way anyone feels angry' " (pp.84-85).

9.   The following body of work, originated by Richard D. Lane, on the "Levels of emotional awareness scale" (LEAS) is recommended for consultation:
        Lane RD, Schwartz GE. "Levels of emotional awareness: a cognitive-developmental theory and its application to psychopathology." Am J Psychiatry. 1987 Feb;144(2):133-43; "The authors present a cognitive-developmental theory of emotional awareness that creates a bridge between normal and abnormal emotional states. Their primary thesis is that emotional awareness is a type of cognitive processing which undergoes five levels of structural transformation along a cognitive-developmental sequence derived from an integration of the theories of Piaget and Werner. The five levels of structural transformation are awareness of bodily sensations, the body in action, individual feelings, blends of feelings, and blends of blends of feelings. ..."
        [Note, however, that the LEAS, a twenty-item self-report performance test takes at least thirty minutes for a patient to complete, not

counting whatever number of minutes the clinician needs to score it. A four-item shorter LEAS was developed by Claudia Subic-Wrana and Jörg Wiltink (see below, Subic-Wrana et al, 2014). In any case, both versions of the LEAS focus on reducing a patient's answers to a numeric score, while the PDMQ focuses on retaining a patient's actual words, which might well convey considerably more clinical information about a unique, individual patient. It easily could be argued that the PDMQ represents a more practical approach for the average clinician – especially in a somewhat emergent setting.]

Lane RD, Quinlan DM, Schwartz GE, Walker PA, Zeitlin SB. "The levels of emotional awareness scale: a cognitive-developmental measure of emotion." J Pers Assess. 1990 Fall;55(1-2):124-34.

Subic-Wrana C, Beutel ME, Garfield DA, Lane RD. "Levels of emotional awareness: a model for conceptualizing and measuring emotion-centered structural change." Int J Psychoanal. 2011 Apr;92(2):289-310; "...The LEA model conceptualizes a basic psychological capacity, affect processing. As we will illustrate using two case vignettes, by operationalizing implicit and explicit modes of affect processing, it provides a clinical measure of emotional awareness that is highly pertinent to the ongoing psychoanalytic debate on the nature and mechanisms of structural change."

Subic-Wrana C, Beutel ME, Brähler E, Stöbel-Richter Y, Knebel A, Lane RD, Wiltink J. "How is emotional awareness related to emotion regulation strategies and self-reported negative affect in the general population?" PLoS One. 2014 Mar 17;9(3):e91846; "...Our first findings suggest that conscious awareness of emotions may be a precondition for the use of reappraisal as an adaptive emotion regulation strategy. They encourage further research in the relation between subconscious and conscious emotional awareness and the preference of adaptive or maladaptive emotion regulation strategies. ..."

#

ERRONEOUS
PSYCHIATRIC
SELF-DIAGNOSIS

:

Non-Psychiatric Patients that
Present at a Psychiatrist's Office

:

[WITH EXTENSIVE BIBLIOGRAPHIES]

FREUDIAN
CONCEPTS IN
AMERICA

:

THE ROLE OF
PSYCHICAL RESEARCH IN
PREPARING THE WAY

:

1904-1934

WHEN DEATH
IS NOT
THEORETICAL

:

The Readiness of the
Music Group 'Queen' for
Living with Freddie
Mercury's Dying

www.ingramcontent.com/pod-product-compliance
Lightning Source LLC
Chambersburg PA
CBHW030551290526
45786CB00004B/1969